The Feminine Abject in Contemporary Art:

Pipilotti Rist, Helen Chadwick, and Adrian Piper

Georgia Legg

An imprint of Boom Publications Ltd

272 Bath Street
Glasgow SCOTLAND
G2 4JR

Boom Graduates and the logo are trademarks of Boom Publications Ltd.

Boom Publications Ltd is a more-than-profit company, dedicating over half our profits to university scholarships for underprivileged students worldwide. In order to offset our carbon footprint, we also pledge to plant a tree for each graduation book commissioned.

The Feminine Abject in Contemporary Art
was first published in Great Britain in 2022.

Copyright © Georgia Legg. Georgia Legg has asserted her right under the
Copyright, Designs and Patents Act, 1988,
to be identified as Author of this work.
For legal purposes any Acknowledgements constitute
an extension of this copyright page.
Cover design by Boom Graduates Ltd and the Book Cover Zone USA.

All rights are reserved. No part of this publication may be reproduced or transmitted in any form or by any means, electronic or mechanical, including photocopying, recording, or any information storage or retrieval system, without prior permission in writing from the publishers.

Boom Publications Ltd do not have any control over, or responsibility for any third-party websites referred to or in this book. All internet addresses given in this book were correct at the time of going to press. The author and publisher regret any inconvenience if addresses have changed or sites have ceased to exist, but can accept no responsibility for any such changes.

Typeset by Helen at Boom Graduates.
Printed and bound in the UK.

To find out more about our authors and books visit www.boomgraduates.com
and sign up for our newsletters.

The Feminine Abject in Contemporary Art

Georgia Legg

Contents

Author biography 7
Abstract 9
List of Figures 13
Introduction 15
The Feminine Abject 25
Pipilotti Rist, 'Sip my Ocean', 1996 31
Helen Chadwick, 'Loop My Loop', 1991 41
Adrian Piper, 'Catalysis', 1970-1973 51
Conclusion 63
References 67
Author's acknowledgements 71
A note about Boom Graduates 73
BOOM! 77
Notes 79

Georgia Legg

Author biography

Georgia Legg holds a First Class BA (Hons) in Fine Art from the Duncan of Jordanstone College of Art and Design (DJCAD), University of Dundee. During her time studying Georgia developed an interest in contemporary feminist art. Her research focuses on the challenging stereotypical perceptions of the female body, and the political and social differences women often experience throughout their lives. To further develop her writing and research skills during her studies Georgia published articles in both the *Dundee University Review of the Arts* and *The Meridian Magazine*. Georgia was also a recipient of the In-GEAR Publishing Awards 2022 at the University of Dundee. With the skills developed during her undergrad she has progressed onto the MFA Art & Humanities course at DJCAD to develop and advance the work in this book.

Georgia Legg

Abstract

This book investigates a fascination into the feminine abject in contemporary art. Through the lens of critical theory, this body of research has involved conducting analysis into works by artists Pipilotti Rist, Helen Chadwick, and Adrian Piper. An objective of this book is, through research into these selected feminist contemporary artists, to question if we have the ability to feel supposedly opposing emotions simultaneously while viewing their work.

The first chapter sets out the groundwork needed to fully understand the topic, defining Julia Kristeva's (1980) theory into abjection in relation to art and the wider world through the progress of history. This is done through referencing St. Augustine's (1790) biblical writings on beauty and disgust, and by analysing the history of sexism in advertisement, in addition to scientific investigation into the topic.

The second chapter investigates Pipilotti Rist's work titled 'Sip My Ocean' (1996) and considers what are called 'female conditions' such as madness and Victorian hysteria, together with reference to mermaid folklore relating this to castration anxiety and voyeuristic pleasure.

The third chapter explores Helen Chadwick's 'Loop My Loop' (1991), through archival research, to examine her use of unconventional materials relating to sexual desire and feminism, relating back to the use of mourning jewellery in the Nineteenth Century.

The fourth chapter focuses on Adrian Piper's series called 'Catalysis' (1970-73) which examines questions on race, culture, society and misogyny, and how this work challenges social structures in its use of excess and discusses female beauty as a vortex of emotions.

Finally, this book concludes with a reflection on the question raised and issues a developed opinion on whether or not through contemporary feminine abject art, can more than one contradictory feeling in the viewer be felt concurrently.

Georgia Legg

List of Figures

Figure 1

Helen Chadwick, *Loop My Loop*, 1991, Cibachrome transparency, glass, steel, electrical apparatus, 127x76x15cm, edition of 3.

Copyright Estate of the Artist, Courtesy Richard Saltoun Gallery London and Rome.

Georgia Legg

Introduction

Now then, we find ourselves in quite the cultural predicament and it would seem there is an imminent need for change as our little planetary rock hurtles towards a species-altering dilemma, which manifests itself in post-humanist theory and is engineered by the influence of artificial intelligence (AI). Technology is at the forefront of these developments and is grossly prevalent in society already today so to imagine a future entirely dictated by computer algorithms, combined with the introduction of human symbiosis with machine, augmented and in an interplanetary environment, is not too difficult to understand - even more so if you have ever watched or read any science fiction material.

Posthumanism is a multi-disciplined ideal that explores the possibilities of what it will mean for humanity when we reach a state of becoming "beyond-human" and by doing so it attempts to imagine how the world may look in a future where we have reached a point of cultural advancement via our integration with AI. This is very similar to the Transhumanist movement that hopes to go one step further and download consciousness into a synthetic organism before discarding of its human remains.

Will we still be human? Are we already "Posthuman?" To be able to understand the underlying currents behind such theories, we must firstly understand the notions that precede the concept and the humanist ideologies that inspired the Renaissance movement, why this still influences modern times, and how it relates to the present topic. We must weigh it up against the comparisons of the world nowadays, as we brace ourselves for a new utopian future imagined by tech giants and billionaire colonialists such as Bill Gates (Microsoft), Jeff Bezos (Amazon) and Elon Musk (Tesla).

The human advancement in belief and consciousness which transcended during the Renaissance period saw a momentous surge in artistic and cultural endeavours, epitomised by historical works from the likes of Leonardo

Da Vinci (1452-1519), Michelangelo (1475-1564), Raphael (1483-1520), and Caravaggio (1571-1610) - each attaining a legendary level of craftmanship in an era still celebrated today as the birth of the classical arts, but this cultural shift also came at a cost and with blood on its hands… the blood of colonial conquests that aimed to spread the ideology of a rejuvenated Western society which devoured everything in its path, changing the course of history forever.

> *They always say time changes things, but you actually have to change them yourself. Progress is impossible without change, and those who cannot change their minds cannot change anything. If we don't change, we don't grow. If we don't grow, we aren't really living.*
>
> *- Aristotle 384 BC – 322 AD*

Greek philosopher Aristotle explains to us that time itself cannot change our reality but instead, that it is down to us to affect that change within ourselves – firstly, because if we cannot accomplish this, then we shall never grow, we will never attain our full potential and we will never really be truly alive. Fast forward to these modern times and it is now a concept that echoes eerily in the distance but is still as applicable today as it was back then, where we are charted on course to a technological singularity that will question our very humanity and seek to achieve the proposed metamorphic advancement needed to fully usher in the posthuman/transhuman phase of our evolutionary process.

To change often is to be perfect. Such an ideology could be applied to any scenario or dilemma, from the minor issues like my art practice to the anthropocentric conundrum we are experiencing today but the theory is exceptionally adept in relation to issues like the global warming crisis, overpopulation, and the need to secure a sustainable future. But how these changes may come into realisation is not elementary for you, nor I, but for the billionaire colonialists and corporations who are leading the charge ahead into the future with innovations that are ready to combine man and machine. These aspire for us to be living in utopian colonies, and have some even predicting the possibility that immortality is now on the table.

The Feminine Abject in Contemporary Art

These topics have been the focus of many renowned writers, philosophers, and artists over the years, and the echoes of the Renaissance period still leave a lot to be explored - but my aim for the moment is to help you to better understand the moral, cultural, and philosophical repercussions of these crusades of enlightenment and the colonial consequences of aggressive capitalist progression so that we can begin to discuss how artists can adapt to the situation, as the world experiences a shunt into further digital dependence and how we can move forward into the future - in acknowledgement, that change is an inevitably not to be feared but to be embraced.

Posthumanism has recently been a growing area of important research, as demonstrated by a search of the British Library's thesis collection (see for example, Wilde 2016, Chkhaidz 2021 and Wilson Hughes 2021) but there is no significant research into how artists can navigate the coming developments, nor on how this transition can be achieved, to ensure that we can continue to positively influence any shift in culture. Although, the area has been written and researched extensively by many before myself, there appears to be a significant gap in knowledge that needs to be addressed sooner rather than later - so it is my intention to further explore these issues in the hope of presenting a platform for future scholarly activity.

The research and ideas that will be discussed directly affect my own art practice, as technology has been integrated into my work during the past year of coronavirus lockdowns. However, it has also further enhanced my creative dexterity so therefore, my own ideas of being an artist have already been severely affected. There had to be an adaptation to the transformations presented before us, and we will soon learn that disruption is the key to change.

As artists prepare for the end of their studies and step into professional practice, the drive towards digital integration has become overbearingly apparent, which at times has left me questioning my practice because times are changing, the arts are changing and the need for artists are changing. With the recent trend of digital arts and non-fungible tokens (NFTs), creatives at all levels have been put on notice that the traditional arts days of glory and dominance may be at an end, as crypto gets cultural.

The Feminine Abject in Contemporary Art

This book investigates the fascination of the feminine abject in contemporary art practice through critical theory, of works by the feminist artists Pipilotti Rist (b.1962), Helen Chadwick (1953-96) and Adrian Piper (b.1948).

The objective of this research is to examine how selected feminist artists use the human body and its bodily functions in abject ways to investigate conflicting feelings, and whether or not we have the capacity to feel differing emotions simultaneously.

The key issues that will be discussed are how contemporary artists use the theory of the abject in their work to show a contrast between disgust and desire, and whether these obviously contradictory feelings can be felt at the same time. This is achieved through looking into ancient biblical writings by St Augustine and at one-point diagnosable conditions such as scopophilia and hysteria. The topic will be investigated by looking at theorists, historians, philosophers and art critics with interests in this area. These include, Julia Kristeva (b.1941), Jack Holland (1947-2004), Laura Mulvey (b.1941), Immanuel Kant (1724-1804), Sigmund Freud (1856-1939) and Roland Barthes (1915-1980). As well as looking into theories from other disciplines, for example, research has also been conducted into scientific psychology papers to develop a well-rounded investigation. Archival sources at the Henry Moore Institute, Leeds, England, were further examined, to further advance this research.

This research area is relevant to my own creative practice as a main aim in my artistic work is to distort the viewer's perception of the human body. I work to examine the body through its skin, orifices, tissues and fluids, creating an intense juxtaposition between what is seen as beautiful and grotesque.

This research is particularly important today as through social media and advertising, we have changed the way we view the human body. Through photoshopped and highly filtered photos we are being exposed to unrealistic beauty standards and expectations. Through a distorted, misleading depiction of (mainly) the female form, we are creating an unachievable 'perfection'.

This book is formed of four chapters. Chapter one, 'The Feminine Abject' discusses and describes the word 'abject' and how it fits into wider literature, history and human nature, while also linking to the 'feminine'. It will introduce why 'grotesque' art is a crucial genre in art and how it links to abjection. To do this, I discuss the definition of 'Scopophilia' in relation to how we look at and view art. Finally in chapter one I start to investigate the overriding question of whether or not opposing feelings can be felt at the same time when viewing art.

In chapter two, on Pipilotti Rist 'Sip My Ocean' (1996), I begin by introducing the artwork and give a description of the artists' intentions. I then go on to link the work to 'hysteria' and how this is usually branded as a female attribute, but also how this could contradict the beauty in the work, thus creating strongly opposing emotions and connotations. I show how feminine stereotypes are often shown to become monstrous, showing a link between female desire and repulsion.

Furthermore, in chapter three, Helen Chadwick 'Loop My Loop' (1991), I again start by introducing the artwork and the artist herself, and what her initial intentions where with the work, which is done here by looking into archival resources. Obvious observations and what theorists and critics in the subject area think will be discussed, linking back to historical traditions of mourning jewellery.

Chapter 4, Adrian Piper 'Catalysis' (1970-73), starts by introducing the works and the artist, and I again discuss the artists' initial intentions. A discussion into judgment surrounding race and class in correlation to the feminist art movement will be considered. Research into bringing abjection into the public sphere and breaking down boundaries of sexism and racism is explored.

This book concludes with a summary under conclusion, in which reflections are made in relation to the question of feeling conflicting emotions in connection to feminine abject art.

The Feminine Abject

Philosopher and psychoanalyst Julia Kristeva (1941) was one of the first to write and define the idea of the 'abject' and its interrelation with existence and the development of individual autonomy. In her book *Powers of Horror: An Essay on Abjection* published in 1980, Kristeva described abjection as 'what disturbs identity, system, order. What does not respect borders positions, rules. The in-between, the ambiguous, the composite' (Kristeva, 1980, p. 4). Kristeva often demonstrates the notion by referring to human materials, such as excrement, blood, saliva, hair, sperm, mucus, and rotting flesh. These are all supposed disgusting bodily materials that we often want to reject, suppress and regulate. Kristeva often explains how these substances can be used to challenge the security of the human subject. This can be seen further when linking to historic biblical writings by St Augustine, bishop and prolific writer.

Augustine was concerned with breaking away from bodily desires. In the renowned book by Jack Holland entitled *A Brief History of misogyny: The World's Oldest Prejudice* published in 2006, Holland writes about the fact that Augustine had a complicated mindset when it came to women. Quoting that :

> He did not see women as inherently evil. In *The City of God,* he stressed that "the sex of woman is not a vice but nature." But the terrible anguish of his struggle with desire, which he records with such power, reveals clearly that it is man's battle with himself that is at the root of misogyny (Holland, 2006, p. 94).

This 'battle' with desire Augustine writes about, links back to Kristeva's idea of the use of offensive bodily materials which forces us to challenge our perception of what we lust over. This view of women can be seen in our everyday lives through how we have perceived and used women in advertisement over time. Over the decades, media advertisement has projected unrealistic, sexualised and stereotyped roles of the female and the female body. "Sex sells" is one of the oldest advertisement sayings. The origin goes as far back as the 1880s when a tobacco company used sexualised depictions of women in their advertisements to sell cigarettes (Padilla, 2019). This overabundant view and objectification of women in advertisement has naturally shaped how not only women view their own body, but also, how specifically heterosexual men perceive and treat women.

Kristeva was often inspired by French psychoanalyst Jacques Lacan's 1936 theory of the "mirror stage" where an infant is first exposed to an external image of the body through a reflection - and the work of French philosopher Georges Bataille's selected writings, 1927-1939. Kristeva's work suggests that this term could transgress beyond a person - to the equivocal space between oneself and the "other" which could potentially jeopardise the capacity to be one's own person (McGhie, 2009). According to the Oxford Dictionary (2021) femininity is defined by a 'Feminine quality; the characteristic quality or assemblage of qualities pertaining to the female sex, womanliness; in early use also, female nature'. This shows how the definition of being feminine has evolved over time. This could be in relation to the radical and cultural feminist movements of the 1960s and 1970s. Many feminist artists of this time created strikingly rebellious work that were an attempt to fight against a typical patriarchal view of how females should act, the work then often exploring the body's "interior" (McGhie, 2009). Art Historian Lynda Nead (b.1957) once described the link of the feminine with the abject in her book *The Female Nude: Art, Obscenity and Sexuality*. She writes 'for Kristeva the abject is on the side of the feminine; it stands in opposition to patriarchal, rule bound order of the symbolic' (Nead, 1992, p. 32).

Artwork that can be described as abject can also often be described as grotesque. Art historian Frances S Connelly described the word 'Grotesque' in her book *The Grotesque in Western Art and Culture* published in 2012, as a "boundary creature" that 'roams the borderline of all that is familiar and controversial' (Connelly, 2012, p. 1). Connelly explains that grotesque art can be seen as more than a subject matter or a choice of genre and style, as it allows for a conversation into matters of humanistic debate and the nature of human beings. Indeed, the grotesque may be an imperative urge of the modern generation.

Theorist Laura Mulvey wrote in her well-known essay 'Visual Pleasure and the Narrative Cinema' (1975) that much of prevailing cinema incorporates and shows Sigmund Freud's concept of "scopophilia", which he wrote about in his book *Three Essays on the Theory of Sexuality* published in 1905. "Scopophilia" has been described as an aesthetic pleasure and curiosity in looking and being looked at - specifically looking at the nude body, fetishes and objects of eroticism. In relation to the abject and use of intimate human materials in artworks, this visual pleasure described can be seen.

When it comes to abject art, feelings such as disgust, horror, and repulsion are felt. But often when this is linked to femininity such feelings can also be seen as beautiful, alluring, and attractive. Undoubtingly these are contradicting feelings. Psychologists have often questioned our ability to experience conflicting emotions at the same time. Author and Doctor of Psychology Leon F. Seltzer wrote that feeling opposite emotions however paradoxical is a logical way of *being* in certain situations. He wrote: 'We've all found ourselves in a push/pull situation' (Seltzer, 2014). Seltzer addresses that feeling trapped between clashing emotions when presented with something, could leave us with a dubious instinct to approach, yet at the same time, stay away. This reflects a great deal of research into abjection and the idea of being attracted and repulsed at the same time.

The following chapters focus on the artworks of three female artists: Pipilotti Rist, Helen Chadwick, and Adrian Piper who all express aspects of feminism, the abject, beauty, and the grotesque within their respective works - all from a range of approaches and methods. All three artists use different mediums, materials and ways of viewing to achieve this.

The Feminine Abject in Contemporary Art

Pipilotti Rist, 'Sip my Ocean', 1996

Pipilotti Rist is a Swiss visual artist born in 1962 ,who is known for her video art and impressive installations. Rist creates immersive environments that allow the viewers to ingulf themselves into a rainbow of projections which often have a preoccupation with the female form. Rist's interests focus on the human body, nature and technology. Her work is often described as intimate, dreamlike and conceptual. She is also regularly cited as being a feminist artist. What is considered feminist art has always been up for debate - when looking into the artists discussed in this book, my understanding is that feminist art investigates and challenges both political and social differences between men and women. Through my research it has become clear that there is a considerable difference between what is described as someone's 'sex' and their 'gender'. 'Sex' refers to how a person is biologically defined and assigned at birth. Whereas 'gender' is described as how a person identifies, and their internal sense of self.

In 1996 Rist created a work called 'Sip My Ocean', a video projected onto two adjacent walls that created a reflecting, mirrored affect. The video consisted of changing views of a man and a woman swimming underwater in shallow clear waters. The woman is wearing a coral dress and then she changes into a yellow bikini. The video is shown in fragmented shots - objects and kids' toys come into view and then sink to the ocean floor – we see teacups and toy caravans fall to the depths (Bullock, 2017). The video is played alongside audio of Rist singing a cover of Chris Isaak's song 'Wicked Game'. She starts by gently humming and singing the song creating a calm atmosphere, but then proceeds to scream the lyrics. This in addition to the visual imagery, challenges our views of voyeurism and femininity. Such subjects have been an ongoing theme in Rist's work. She discussed earlier on in her career, 'I was trying to accept hysteria in myself and in others as a survival tactic. I wanted to explode into pieces and not be ashamed of that' (Rist, 2017). Rist was trying to "accept" her hysteria and intentionally have this be a factor in her work, when often female artists get branded as 'mad' in a discriminatory and biased way. In the book *Women Can't Paint: Gender, The Glass Ceiling and Values in Contemporary Art* by Helen Gørrill published in 2020, she sates, 'The word "hyster" is Latin for 'womb' and so the malady of the womb, "hysteria" is a gender-specific disease that can only affect women' (Gørrill, 2020, p. 148). The use of referring to hysteria as a "disease", when as of 1980 "hysteria" was no longer a diagnosable condition (Cherry, 2020), still allows us to see it as something potentially contagious with symptoms, which Rist attempts to show through the sound in her work. This view also links us back to Kristeva's idea of the abject as being something sickly.

Seduction, Voyeurism, Aggression & Distortion

The vast projection work 'Sip My Ocean' has been described by Natasha Bullock, author and curator of an exhibition of the same name - including this work - as 'a pulsating underwater paradise' (Bullock, 2017). In the same vein, the work has also been described as 'a video projection of a mermaid-like women swimming in paradisical waters who transforms herself into a grotesque figure' by art historian Christine Ross (2001). Both Ross and Bullock describe the work as a somewhat "paradise" when first observed. This shows the primary perception of the work is a calm, pleasant sort of bliss. This is further recognised when Ross goes on to describe the women in the work as "mermaid-like", allowing us to connect our stereotypical perception of mermaids as being beautiful and graceful compared to how we see the women in the work. Mermaids can also have connotations in some cultures to the issue fertility, being bearers of life (Anon., 2021). But this, in connection with neurologist Sigmund Freud's theory of castration anxiety, a fear of loss or damage of the genital organ in boys is seen as punishment for desiring the mother figure, the "bearers of life". This turns mother figures into monsters, just as we see in Rist's work.

Film theorist Laura Mulvey wrote in her book *Visual and Other Pleasures* published in 1989, that 'Masculine castration anxiety inflicts scopophilic pleasure towards misogyny. It activates the fetishistic aspects of voyeuristic pleasure, in which the female form has the allure and threat' (Mulvey, 1989, pp. xi-xii). Again, this references a sometimes-physical attraction, even when dangerous or when a threat is present. Further evidence of this is that in other cultures, mermaids represent a destructive nature of the sea, enchanting sailors to their deaths. This worldwide folklore builds upon the grotesque we see in abject art. In the book by Frances Connelly entitled *The Grotesque in Western Art and Culture*, they expand on this, writing:

> ... torn between fascination and dread. The grotesque too, provokes responses as contradictory as its meanings, fusing humour with horror, wit with transgression, repulsion with desire. Like a minotaur, a mermaid, or a cyborg, the grotesque is not quite one thing or the other (Connelly, 2012, p. 1).

This suggests often how viewing something grotesque alone can stir up a range of emotions.

These legends only add to the speculation in Barbara Creed's book *The Monstruous-Feminine* published in 1993. Here, Creed notes that critics have often ignored that in many film genres the feminine is represented not as a victim or heroine but as a "monster" of sorts (Peters, 1994). This indicates the female figure could be argued as being the abject personified. This is then advanced upon when Ross describes the women in the work each becoming 'a grotesque figure'. This suggests that through the distorted view we have of the women in the video, combined with the progressively disturbing way Rist sings, this enables her to turn into an unpleasant and disgusting creature. This links back again, to the idea of hysteria being a female attribute, and suggests that unless women are kept under control, they are likely to break out into uncontrollable behaviour and be deemed mad. This could start to suggest there is a fine line between attraction and disgust, and that these feelings could be felt simultaneously.

This theory is then challenged by the German philosopher Immanuel Kant in his book *Critique of Judgment,* published in 1790. He claims that ugliness and beauty are outright opposites and completely contradict one another. Kant believed that something disgusting could not at the same time be appealing (Thomson, 1992, pp. 107-115). The idea of something repulsive also being alluring simply was not a possibility according to some scholars (Kant, 1790). Rist's work often disproves this speculation.

Furthermore, curator of exhibition also titled 'Sip My Ocean' Natasha Bullock goes on to claim that Rist's use of lavish, intense colour and captivating music surround the viewer. Her use of reflecting and kaleidoscopic imagery presents our impulse for desire: 'It is a serenade about an impossible wish to not fall in love again and to be in synchronicity with the other' (Bullock, 2017). This view reflects the idea of the abject being both beautiful and repulsive at the same time, the viewers want to walk away and "not fall in love again", but find themselves unable to pull away. This idea reflects the choice of song Rist has chosen to accompany the work, the lyrics in the song also echo this, "I don't want to fall in love" and "Strange what desire will make foolish people do" (Isaak, 1989). This is further commented upon when Bullock writes, 'Her work shows [both] the interconnectedness between being emotionally up and down, of being mild and agitated' and 'Feelings of hysteria and pleasure are pronounced' – suggesting that when viewing Rist's work, the viewer is taken on a roller-coaster of contradicting feelings and emotions.

Again, in Laura Mulvey's book *Visual and Other Pleasures* she writes about situations where looking can be a source of pleasure in itself, and that there is pleasure in being looked at. This was researched in Freud's 'Three Essays on Sexuality' published in 1905 where he outlined scopophilia as one of the fundamental impulses of sexuality (Freud, 1905). 'Scopophilia' has been defined in psychology and psychiatry, as a voyeuristic pleasure of looking at a subject or an object. This term is often used when discussing the male gaze in Hollywood cinema, in which women on the screen are simply there to be looked at by men. Rist creates an immense but also intimate space showing herself and her body for viewers to contemplate and stare at, being an object of pleasure and curious gaze. Mulvey also goes on to distinguish a "sexual imbalance" writing that the pleasure of looking can be divided in two, the "active/male and passive/female" (Mulvey, 1989). Furthermore, she argues the active, voyeuristic position can be described as "masculine" whereas the passive, women's body is seen and described as the "other". This suggests that Rist as the "object" in the work is shown to be actively looked at by the male, and thus have their voyeuristic fantasies projected onto her accordingly.

Georgia Legg

Helen Chadwick, 'Loop My Loop', 1991

Helen Chadwick, 1953-1996, was a British conceptual artist best known for her sculptures and photography. In 1987 Chadwick became one of the first women artists to ever be nominated for the Turner Prize. Chadwick's work has often been described as having aesthetic beauty but being created out of unconventional, often grotesque and vile materials. Her work was well known to challenge stereotypes with a strong focus on the human body, often drawing inspiration from science and unconventional and bizarre materials. She was interested in exploring binary opposites in her work and dissolving boundaries relating to sexuality, often linking to feminism. Chadwick's work frequently focused on the female body in relation to an array of objects and materials. She explored identity through these and often depicted her own body in her work.

Chadwick made a significant work called 'Loop My Loop' in 1991 (fig.1, below). A back-lit tableau in which long strands of blonde hair are interwoven with pig's intestines, was photographed as a modern dramatic still-life.

Here, Chadwick immediately disturbs our outlook, by combining one of the most outright symbols we associate with beauty, with something, when out of context, that is grotesque and hideous. Hair is repeatedly linked with one's virility, beauty and femininity and can be seen as a symbol of specifically female seduction and physical attraction. This next to the pig's intestines, however, causes a large juxtaposition of what is viewed as "natural" beauty. In St Augustine's *Confessions,* consisting of 13 books written between AD 397 and 400, Augustine asks in *Book IV* "What is beauty?". What about beauty entices him, as if there is no outward 'beauty' women "could by no means draw us into them" (Augustine, AD 397-400).

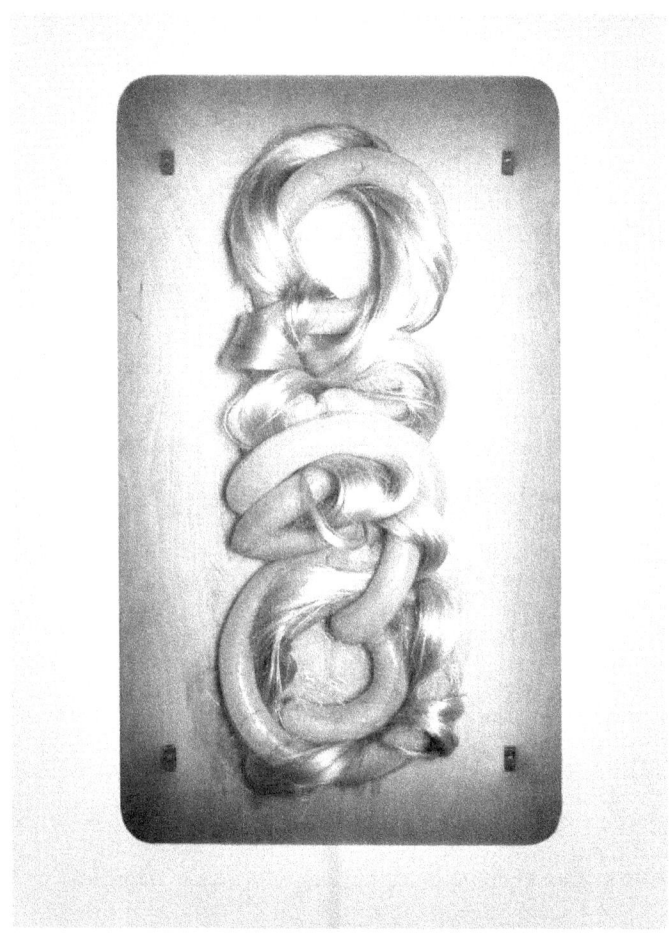

Fig. 1. Helen Chadwick, *Loop My Loop*, 1991, Cibachrome transparency, glass, steel, electrical apparatus, 127x76x15cm, edition of 3, Copyright Estate of the Artist, Courtesy Richard Saltoun Gallery London and Rome.

Augustine's statements bring attention to what Chadwick tried to challenge in her work, having the viewer of the work question what we define as beautiful.

Horrifyingly Seductive Juxtaposition

Conceptual artist Helen Chadwick often challenged unusual and bodily taboos in her work. She frequently used unpleasant and disgusting materials, such as urine, rotting vegetables and flesh, as subject matter for her photographs and sculptures. Much of Chadwick's most famous works show a fine line between what can be seen as vulgar and beautiful. With the use of bodily materials and fluids she created aesthetically amusing sculptures.

The work 'Loop My Loop' presents gold locks of hair and pink pig intestines. Human hair is often a form of identity and seen specifically as feminine, meaning it is frequently fetishised and sexualised (Ellery, 2014). But in this work Chadwick links us to ideas of death and repulsion by introducing the intestines, meaning to disrupt our concepts of what is appealing and beautiful. Hair and specifically human hair is something Chadwick frequently drew inspiration from in her work.

When looking in her handwritten notebooks which are archived at the Henry Moore Institute in Leeds, England, we can clearly see this. They contain comprehensive notes, sketches, doodles and ideas that all show an insight into Chadwick's mind - when researching and brainstorming before, and during, the making of her early works. Reference to hair can be found all through these notebooks, for example, she wrote, "Hair: shaving, cutting/trimming, Plucking, Curling, Brushing, combing, Cleaning, shampooing" and "wigs + shaving of body hair" (Chadwick, 1975-78, courtesy the Henry Moore Institute). This shows that hair was a constant inspiration to Chadwick, and she would often make lists and notes showing this.

The use of intestines in the work confuses our assumptions of feminine beauty. Regardless of the fact that both are organic materials, we regard the animal's internal organ as extremely grotesque and hard to look at. This work brings up many binary opposites such as pleasure and disgust, organic and manmade - meaning when viewing the work our opinions are always going back and forth through stark opposites. Through the use of human hair, Chadwick is confronted with gendered stereotypes regarding beauty and desire, and challenges their well-known patterns in society. There are also certain links that connect this work to mourning jewellery made in the Eighteenth Century, in which women created small pieces of sentimental jewellery that incorporated the hair from a dead loved one. This use of hair to represent a deceased loved one in mourning jewellery could suggest that the hair in 'Loop My Loop' operates as a depiction of seductive voyeurism. In mourning jewellery, the use of hair is present to show that death is permanent, whereas in 'Loop My Loop', it analyses the projection of sexual desire of female bodies. This references again what St Augustine questions in his confession books, the difference between the inside and outside of a women's body. They have eternal beauty on the outside and potentially have an ugly soul on the inside (Dugas, 2018). Also, there is a repulsion to what unknown lies inside. In both, hair becomes innate and confusing (Scott, 2020). Chadwick then proceeded to intertwine the hair with pink, flesh like pig intestines, making it extremely difficult to separate anything attractive or feminine with the grotesque fetishised certainty of death. Chadwick's work was massively influenced by many writers, including George Bataille, the French philosopher and writer of *Visions of Excess: Selected Writings, 1927 – 1939*, in which he wrote about our ingrained and compelling attraction to the repulsive and ugly (Bataille, 1985).

'Loop My Loop' has been described as 'a horrifyingly seductive juxtaposition' (Scott, 2020). This statement could suggest that this work could be seen as both attractive and grotesque at the same time. When describing the idea of the abject in art, Julia Kristeva explains that a reaction to something abject could be interpreted as a kind of "vortex" (Willette, 2013), meaning that the viewers' feelings could go round in circles with no conclusive answer - that the abject can entice you, repulse you and then entice you again, like a whirlpool of reflecting emotions. On the other hand, to argue against this, Immanuel Kant stated in his book *Observations of the Feeling of the Beautiful and Sublime* published in 1764 that, 'Nothing is so opposed to the beautiful as the disgusting, just as nothing sinks more deeply beneath the sublime than the ridiculous' (Kant, 1764, p. 40). This suggests that when something is visual or has connotations to being "beautiful" that the idea of feeling "disgust" towards that, is not possible. This implies that when disgust is felt when viewing 'Loop My Loop', it is not possible to then see any beauty, that the feeling of disgust masks any feelings of attraction that may have been there.

When we look at a work of art depending on who we are – taking into account our life experience, our knowledge and our own thoughts on life - we will read that work on an individual basis. Often when the public views a piece of art, they will base their opinions on what they are seeing, rather than the artists' initial intentions. This reflects the theory written about in 1967 by French theorist Roland Barthes in his essay 'The Death of the Author' in which he wrote 'The birth of the reader must be at the cost of the death of the author' (Barthes, 1967, p. 148). This statement implies, in terms of an artwork, that no matter the intentions of the artist, when it leaves their studio and is viewed in an art gallery, the meaning and message in the work is given over to the person interpreting the art. This important paper will be discussed in more detail in the next chapter.

Georgia Legg

Adrian Piper, 'Catalysis', 1970-1973

Adrian Piper is an African American, feminist conceptual artist and philosopher from New York. Her work often references politics and identity and offers up often uncomfortable questions about race and culture, which complements her career as a philosopher.

She has often been referred as being a feminist artist as her work often challenges and pushes limits on what is seen as feminine. Piper's work is often disturbing and alluring, and asks the viewer to confront their own truths regarding the society they live in. She is best known for her street performances and paintings but works across disciplines to get her point across.

As a female academic and artist, her work is often interlaced with themes of misogyny and sexism, which enabled her to join a generation of multidisciplinary feminist artists (Bowles, 2011). Piper's use of performance art in the 1970s was radical as the term was only just becoming widely known at the time. This was the same time Piper started distinctly addressing her multiracial background as a driving force in her work (Blumberg, 2015). Piper used performance art to challenge assumptions about social structures, while specifically referencing gender, race and many other prejudices.

'Catalysis', made between 1970 and 1973, was one of Piper's earliest series of street performances. The aim of this work was to test the public which came in proximity with Piper throughout the performance. An ambition of Piper's was to challenge the public's perception of her, while simultaneously showing their judgement towards society and class. This work was a series of performances Piper undertook to bring up gender and race inequality, trying to make that visual. It is a series that would establish the way Piper's work would go on to challenge concepts over her 50+-year career.

The Monstruous Feminine in Public

Adrian Piper once wrote:

> My work is an act of communication, and it's important to me the way what I assert lands, and where it lands within someone who sees it. On the other hand, I also recognize fully and live by the principle that once the work leaves my studio, I cannot control the effects it has (Piper, 2002).

This suggests that Piper is fully aware that her work will be interpreted differently by each viewer but also completely differently sometimes to how she intends. She understands that this is just what happens when a work leaves the studio and is given over to the public. This echoes again the argument made by Roland Barthes in 'The Death of the Author' published in 1967. Barthes argues that interpretation is not retrieved or discovered, that it is an active rather than passive action (Barthes, 1967). Piper allows and acknowledges this, which enables her to be a successful conceptual performance artist.

The figure is almost always present in Piper's work but is shown plainly, and used as a tool to get her point across. In the 'Catalysis' series, Piper's body is used as an object of sculpture and used to show and portray the concept of the work. Each work in this series was a different performance where Piper created public situations, in which the public going about their everyday lives, might have become incorporated into her works. As part of the exhibition Adrian Piper had at the Museum of Modern Art entitled 'Adrian Piper: A Synthesis of Institutions, 1965-2016' exhibited in 2018, a preview press conference took place where Cornelia Butler a co-curator of the exhibition stated:

> The figure interestingly is present throughout the work. I think that's something that makes it quite accessible … whether it's the performing figure … she moves from her body being a body to an object and starts to think of her body as an object of sculpture in the early catalysis works (Butler, 2018).

This suggests that a key component in Piper's early performance works was to involve the public and have them be part of the outcomes of the work. She often did this by challenging and questioning the boundaries of socially acceptable behaviour and documenting what happens when they are pushed.

According to the Tate (2021,) abject art can be described as 'artworks which explore themes that transgress and threaten our sense of cleanliness and propriety particularly referencing the body and bodily functions'. Piper's 'Catalysis' series challenges our sense of cleanliness that is normally just expected, especially in the environments her work is performed.

'Catalysis I' was a performance in which Piper soaked her clothes in rancid and rotten substances for a week before boarding a train in New York during peak hours and joined other commuters on their commute wearing these clothes. Piper used rotting eggs, vinegar and fish oil to saturate her clothes before the performance. Through using her body to stimulate the environment she is in, Piper, a black woman appearing with an unmissable rancid odour, forced fellow commuters to become part of the art whether they actively smelled, looked or overlooked her presence. One of Piper's main objectives with this work was to validate her public presence as a black woman, in a society in which this itself could already be seen as abject. In her work she often addressed this, and the questions of gender and race became central in her work while at the time she was active within a largely, male, Caucasian conceptual art movement. Piper wanted to amplify the public's repulsion and dislike towards her presence, and to make these feelings physical by the use of the rancid smells.

This could be linked to Piper',s African American heritage, specifically discrimination that is often seen against black women's hair. Catherine McCormack discusses this in her book *Women in the Picture: Women, Art and the Power of Looking* published in 2021: 'the unmanageable black women with unmanageable hair who have been suppressed and marginalised'. And 'There have been court cases in the United States about the unfair dismissal of women from work who refuse to cut or straighten their natural hair' (McCormack, 2021, p. 182).

This shows that black women are being wrongly dismissed due to their natural hair. This is further recognised as black women are often accused of having smelly hair due to hair products, which could explain one of the reasons Piper used strong smells to evoke emotions in the viewers of her work.

Misogynoir shows how racism, and, in this case, sexism are unmistakable in black women's day-to-day lives, which is what Piper has made visible to us. Piper described the concept of having the artist being part of the art in her ongoing autobiography, she expressed, 'the immediacy of the artist's presence as artwork/catalysis confronts the viewer with a broader, more powerful, and more ambiguous situation than discrete forms or objects'. (Piper, 1996). Piper's work differs in this way from the other artists and works researched in this book as she brings the abject to communal spaces and in a physical way.

While sitting on the train, Piper started to notice that while she was being successful in repulsing the public sitting around her, she was at the same time enticing and alluring them (Piper, 1972). In the book *Adrian Piper: Race, Gender, and Embodiment* published in 2011 by art historian John Bowles, Piper discussed the interaction during this performance:

> In one of the early pieces [Catalysis I]...I was very passive (just standing there), and they would look at me like they really wanted to fuck me...I hadn't counted on at all, that somehow there could be sexuality in that really revolting make-up (Bowles, 2011, pp. 178-79).

At first Piper was shocked to discover this reaction but decided to play on it in other works in the series, such as in 'Catalysis IV', in which Piper dressed conservatively but stuffed a large white bath towel in her mouth until her cheeks bulged to almost twice their size, allowing the rest to hang down in front of her. She then went on to travel on the bus, subway and the Empire State Building elevator. This action of having the towel stuffed in her mouth was a way of gagging herself. A definition of being gagged is to be prevented to have an opinion or reveal information. As far back as the 19th Century, African American women have been fighting for their civil rights and equality in an often white dominant community (Boukari, 2005). The gagging in this work could be a way to visually show this as Piper is an African American woman. But, on the other hand, gagging could have sexual connotations. In which one partner will have dominance over the other, meaning in this piece that even though Piper is the one creating the work, it is the viewer who has the power. Sexuality and dominance are explored again in 'Catalysis VII'. In this performance, Piper goes to view an exhibition at the Metropolitan Museum wearing stereotypically feminine clothing. She wears high heels, and a short skirt that showed her body more than usual. While walking around the exhibition Piper chewed extensive amounts of gum, blowing large bubbles and allowing them to stick to her face when they popped. Over time the bubbles left her a sticky mess in this pristine museum. During an interview for 'Women in the Arts' Piper stated,

> It looked very strange, and I seemed to be a threat, because if people got entangled in

> that stuff, then they would be involved, and I'd have to have some kind of interaction with them, and obviously they were very much avoiding that.

Again, Piper was trying to make the public's perception of her a physical one by exaggerating her typically feminine characteristics, the pink gum and revealing outfit, but amplified them so much that they became repulsive to view. This idea is once again mentioned in Immanuel Kant's book *Observations of the feeling of the Beautiful and Sublime* in 1764, where he writes 'Nothing is so disgusting as pure sweetness' (Kant, 1764, p. 53). This suggests that stereotypical feminine beauty may only be considered beautiful when done so in moderation, if not it may turn into something that is viewed as disgusting or grotesque. The over-the-top outfit Piper wears, pushes the boundaries of what it is to be feminine, where feminine traits are often described as gentle, modest and tender.

These performances show clearly going from one extreme to the other, going from repulsion to seduction and beauty to disgust. This cycle that Piper projected reflects again the "vortex" theory by Julia Kristeva, of feelings and emotions going round in circles (Kristeva, 1980). This theory can be seen emerging back in 1790 in Immanuel Kant's book *Critique of Judgement*, where he writes 'the object is represented as it were obtruding itself for our enjoyment while we strive against it with all our might' (Kant, 1790, p. 19).

This idea can be seen clearly in Piper's 'Catalysis I' where even though the smell Piper created is so outrageously grotesque and repulsive, it still begs for our attention and draws us in.

Georgia Legg

Conclusion

This book set out to discuss the fascination of the feminine abject in contemporary art. When the term "abjection" is used in a feminist context, it brings up social, political and economic issues. This allows it to be an important and exciting concept in relation to contemporary art.

The abject is a complicated theory about being uncontained and not following rules, developed by philosopher Julia Kristeva (1980). Particularly in the visual arts, the abject commonly involves the use of bodily functions and materials, as well as social structure. This suggests that in general, abject can also be described as grotesque to view.

In the 1980s and 90s many artists became familiar with the term and the theory behind it, and this showed in a great deal of artists' works. Feminising abjection in contemporary art allows time for deeper thought and reflection, into how we perceive beauty and repulsion and how we view women's bodies when presented in this way. All three women artists discussed in this book use the abject as a strategy to reclaim the feminine body and identity that has relentlessly been used as the primary object of sexualisation in a (mainly) heterosexual culture and society.

This study has found that the use of creating grotesque art is to attract attention to the work. This attention can then be interpreted in different ways depending on the individual viewing the art and their previous exposure to the grotesque. Reflecting the theory of Roland Barthes (1967), in relation to art, when an artwork is viewed it is completely up to the viewer to interpretate it and shine their own judgment on it.

The question raised in this dissertation is can two supposedly contradictory feelings such as, repulsion and seduction and something beautiful and grotesque, be viewed and felt at the same time in contemporary feminine abject art? Through researching the opinions of art critics, historians and theorists who specialise in this area, they often come to different conclusions. Throughout this book, seduction, disgust, femininity, the grotesque and sexuality have generated complicated questions about our views surrounding what is classed as beautiful and ugly. St. Augustine (AD 397-400), in questioning "What is beauty?", shows that this debate has been going on for many centuries. The use of the abject in this argument allows us to question what is also classed as ugly or grotesque.

A common factor in all three artist's works is the use of the 'female'. The use of the 'mermaid' like figure in Rist's work, the hair in Chadwick's and the stereotypically feminine features in Piper's work, are all initially viewed as attractive and not repulsive. But through exaggerating the grotesque through abjection, it often alters and shifts our view back and forth creating a confusing viewing experience.

Rist, Chadwick and Piper all set out to reclaim and reimagine the image of the female body. They address beauty, femininity, distortion, sex, seduction and the grotesque, which may be seen as taboo subject matters.

Through critical analysis into contemporary artist's Pipilotti Rist, Helen Chadwick and Adrian Piper, they have indicated that though feelings of disgust and beauty that are felt when viewing their works seem to be complete opposing emotions, it is common to view and feel them alongside each other. According to scientists, many theorists and viewers' comments after viewing their work, it is common to feel a juxtaposition between two contradictory feelings. This is further discussed in Kristeva's (1980) definition of the "vortex" of emotions, that something described as abject, can at once summon and reject you.

As Immanuel Kant (1790) suggests in his writing, disgust is the most hostile opposition to beauty, but through the artwork's researched in this dissertation, this theory is questioned, as these emotions are often viewed together - and potentially - in unison.

References

Ally, M., 2016. *The Meaning and Value of Experiencing Conflicting Emotions,* s.l.: s.n.
Anon., 2017. *Exhibition: Pipilotti Rist Sip My Ocean.* [Online]
Available at: https://www.mca.com.au/artists-works/exhibitions/pipilotti-rist/
[Accessed 12 November 2021].
Anon., 2021. *Royal Museums Greenwich.* [Online]
Available at:
https://www.rmg.co.uk/stories/topics/what-mermaid
[Accessed 27 November 2021].
Anon., n.d. *Sip My Ocean.* [Online]
Available at:
https://www.guggenheim.org/artwork/5208
[Accessed 12 November 2021].
Augustine, S., AD 397-400. *Confessions.* Book IV ed. s.l.:s.n.
Barthes, R., 1967. *The Death of the Author.* s.l.:s.n.
Bataille, G., 1985. *Visions of Excess: Selected Writings: 1927 - 1939.* illustrated ed. s.l.:U of Minnesota Press.
Blumberg, N., 2015. *Adrian Piper: American conceptual and performance artist,* s.l.: Britannica.
Bowles, J. P., 2011. *Adrian Piper: Race, Gender, and Embodiment.* illustrated ed. s.l.:Duke University Press.

Bullock, N., 2017. *Pipilotti Rist: Sip My Ocean.* [Online]
Available at: https://www.mca.com.au/stories-and-ideas/pipilotti-rist-sip-my-ocean-curatorial-essay/
[Accessed 12 November 2021].
Butler, C., 2018. *Adrian Piper: A Synthesis of Intuitions, 1965-2016 MoMA LIVE* [Interview] (31 March 2018).
Chadwick, Helen 1975-78. [notebook]. The Henry Moore Institute Archive. Leeds: HMI
Cherry, K., 2020. *What is Hysteria? The Past and Present,* s.l.: verywell mind.
Connelly, F. S., 2012. *The Grotesque in Western Art and Culture: The Image at Play.* illustrated, reprint ed. s.l.:Cambridge University Press.
Ellery, L., 2014. *Huffpost.* [Online]
Available at: https://www.huffpost.com/entry/hair-history-why-hair-is-_b_5567365
[Accessed 4 April 2021].
Freud, S., 1905. *Three Essays on the Theory of Sexuality.* 240 pages, Paperback ed. s.l.:Verso Books, 2017.
Gørrill, H., 2020. *Women Can't Paint: Gender, The Glass Ceiling and Values in Contemporary Art.* s.l.:Bloomsbury.
Isaak, Chris 1989. [song]. Wicked Game.
Kant, I., 1764. *Observations on the Feeling of the Beautiful and Sublime.* s.l.:s.n.
Kant, I., 1790. *Critique of Judgement.* s.l.:s.n.
Kristeva, J., 1980. *Powers of Horror: An Essay on Abjection.* s.l.:Columbia University Press.
Leon F. Seltzer, P., 2014. *Psychology Today.* [Online]
Available at: https://www.psychologytoday.com/us/blog/evolution-the-self/201406/can-you-feel-two-emotions-once
[Accessed 12 November 2021].

Manchester, E., 2002. *Tate.* [Online]
Available at: https://www.tate.org.uk/art/artworks/chadwick-enfleshings-i-t06876
[Accessed 29 November 2021].

McCormack, C., 2021. *Women in the Picture: Women, Art and the Power of Looking.* illustrated ed. s.l.:Icon Books.

McGhie, H., 2009. *Cindy Sherman and Jo Spence: Monstrousness, Abjection & Female Identity,* s.l.: University of Sunderland.

Mulvey, L., 1989. *Visual and other Plasures.* illustrated ed. s.l.:s.n.

Nead, L., 1992. *The Female Nude: Art, Obscenity and Sexuality.* illustrated, reprint ed. s.l.:Routledge.

Peters, G., 1994. Barbara Creed. The Monstrous-Feminine: Film, Feminism, Psychoanalysis.. *Journals. University of Toronto Press,* 3(2), pp. 108-113.

Piper, A., 1996. Talking to Myself: The Ongoing Autobiography of an Art Object. In: s.l.:s.n., pp. 42-43.

Piper, L. L. &. A., 1972. Catalysis: An Interview with Adrian Piper. *The Drama Review,* Volume 16, pp. 76-78.

Rist, P., 2017. *Pipilotti Rist in conversation with Massimiliano Gioni* [Interview] (19 January 2017).

Ross, C., 2001. *Pipilotti Rist: Images as quasi-objects,* s.l.: s.n.

Ross, C., 2016. *Digicult.* [Online]
Available at: http://digicult.it/articles/art/pipilotti-rist-sip-my-ocean/
[Accessed 12 November 2021].

Scott, E., 2020. *The Decay of the Feminist Aesthetic in Helen Chadwick's Loop My Loop,* s.l.: s.n.

Seltzer, L. F., 2014. *Can You Feel Two Emotions at Once?,* s.l.: Psychology Today.

Vilalta, H., 2019. Becoming Adrian Piper. *Oxford Art Journal,* 42(1), pp. 125-130.
Willette, D. J. S. M., 2013. *Art History Unstuffed.* [Online]
Available at: https://arthistoryunstuffed.com/julia-kristeva-and-abjection/
[Accessed 3 April 2021].

Author's acknowledgements

Firstly, I wish to thank the Richard Saltoun Gallery in London and Rome for their kind permission to use the image of Helen Chadwick, *Loop My Loop*, 1991. I am extremely grateful for your generosity in enabling this important work to be shared.

Thank you to all of the lecturers, tutors, and supervisors that steered me through my degree. Without your generous support and great guidance I wouldn't have been able to explore and develop my interests. I am specifically grateful to Dr Helen Gorrill for being a thoughtful and dedicated supervisor and for showing confidence in my work.

I would also like to acknowledge with gratitude, the continued support and love of all my family. My Dad for all those early morning drop offs, at the train station and my

Mum for always being there to answer all my questions and to guide me though adult life - Thank you.

A note about Boom Graduates

We propel graduates forward so they can make their mark on the world - we push the boundaries, share brilliant ideas and inspire possibility. We publish dissertations as books, presented gift-boxed at graduation ceremonies, delivering brand-new research to the world quicker than anyone else. We plant trees for every commissioned book sold, and give our Boom graduates the chance to profit-share from their brilliant ideas. Furthermore we donate the majority of our profits to funding research and scholarship for disadvantaged students who wouldn't normally be able to attend university. Through academic excellence and environmental sustainability, *Boom Graduates* are changing the world.

We are Boom Graduates - an imprint of Boom Publications Ltd. We are a more-than-profit company, dedicating over half our profits to providing university scholarships for underprivileged students across the world. We aim to become the globe's biggest provider of such scholarships – and if like Georgia, the author of this book, you'd also like to contribute to making the world a better place, please contact us: we publish monographs, edited books, and moreover our graduate series – Boom Graduates – are presented at graduation days across the world in archival, lined museum-quality presentation cases, engraved with the graduate's name and award.

Boom Publications are based at the Duncan of Jordanstone College of Art and Design, at the University of Dundee in Scotland. We were one of the winners of the 2022 Venture awards hosted by the Centre for Entrepreneurship, and have since been shortlisted for the Converge Challenge, a national award that brings together ambitious and creative thinkers with innovative ideas to work with industry experts to transform their ideas into sustainable companies operating in the commercial world. We are also climate conscious and work with agencies to plant a tree for each and every book commissioned, offsetting thousands of tonnes of carbon each year. Follow us on social media to watch our forest grow @boomgraduates.

Thank you for contributing by purchasing this book. Please visit our catalogues on www.boompublications.com.

Georgia Legg

BOOM!

This book was originally submitted as a dissertation in partial fulfilment of the requirements of a Bachelor of Arts (Hons) degree in Fine Art at the Duncan of Jordanstone College of Art and Design, the University of Dundee, in 2022.

Georgia Legg

Notes

Georgia Legg

The Feminine Abject in Contemporary Art

Georgia Legg

The Feminine Abject in Contemporary Art

Georgia Legg

The Feminine Abject in Contemporary Art

Georgia Legg

The Feminine Abject in Contemporary Art

Georgia Legg

The Feminine Abject in Contemporary Art

www.ingramcontent.com/pod-product-compliance
Lightning Source LLC
Chambersburg PA
CBHW051538240526
45465CB00027B/610